Preface

Thank you for purchasing "200 Great Scrapbook Layout Ideas". This book has been created for your enjoyment as well as to increase your creativity for scrapbooking. It contains ideas that range from the very simple to the elaborate. The book has become a reality after a long process of inspiration, prayer and advice from friends.

I want to give special acknowledgments to those wonderful artists who submitted pages for the book, and encouraged me when I thought the book was too big a task for me to publish. A special thanks is due to:

Anita Denson
Ruth Fuller
Missy Gann
DeAnna Lemley
Jodi Long
Jennifer McBride
Deana Olinger
Dean Wilson

This book would not be possible without the exceptional love of my family. My mother, Dean Wilson, introduced me to scrapbooking, and it immediately became my favorite hobby. My husband, John, children, Christina and Daniel have always supported, encouraged and loved me during this stressful endeavor. My father, Thomas Wilson, is always there to support me.

Nancy Simmers of Party Central in Decatur, AL was also a great resource for me.

When you're creating scrapbook pages, I encourage you to not only use stickers and paper, but also include stamping, stenciling, tracing and clipart into your designs. One thing I enjoy in scrapbooking is using all forms of decorating on my pages. Tracing and stenciling can make you look like an artist. Anyone can make scrapbooks, even those of us that can't draw a straight line!

I wish you many happy scrapbooking days in the future.

Dena Crow
Creative Concepts

To reorder, please contact your distributor or
Creative Concepts
Dena Crow
(256) 350-9994

Table of Contents

Holidays

New Year 3
Valentine's Day 4
Easter 5
Father's Day 12
Halloween 13
Christmas 18

Seasons

Winter 29
Summer 30
Fall 37

Miscellaneous

Title Pages 40
Baby 43
Birthday 55
Children 65
School 79
Sports 84
Vacation 86
Wedding 98
Miscellaneous 99

HAPPY
1996
1997
NEW YEAR!

THE NEW YEAR
ONE WAY
IN NEW ORLEANS

Valentines Day

EASTER
Following church, we went to Grandmother &
These eggs are really cute. Libby Ann looks so
pretty in her dress Grandmother
Granddaddy Slatens & MaMa & Granddaddy Marks.
Slaten & Patty Mc made

Easter Morning
Happy Easter
You woke up at 5:00 Easter Morning. It was still dark outside! We came down-stairs to see if the Easter bunny had come. He brought you books, puzzles, toys, and candy. You were very excited and Mommy was very sleepy.

Easter

Our family ate Easter lunch at the Country Club. Katie and Will hunted eggs outside when we were finished eating.

Here you are dying eggs with Katie.
Katie showed us her dance routine. Will did not want to be left out so he started dancing, too.

Easter
Morning
Easter morning, Christina received a basket and a turtle sand box.

EASTER
MY 1st EASTER

Happy
Easter
1996

Chocolate & a Barbie-
Whatmore could a
girl want!!
Easter
Jordan
Kacey
This picture
would be
R-rated if
the basket
was gone!
Abigail, Daddy, Gray, Max & Mamaw Rice
1997

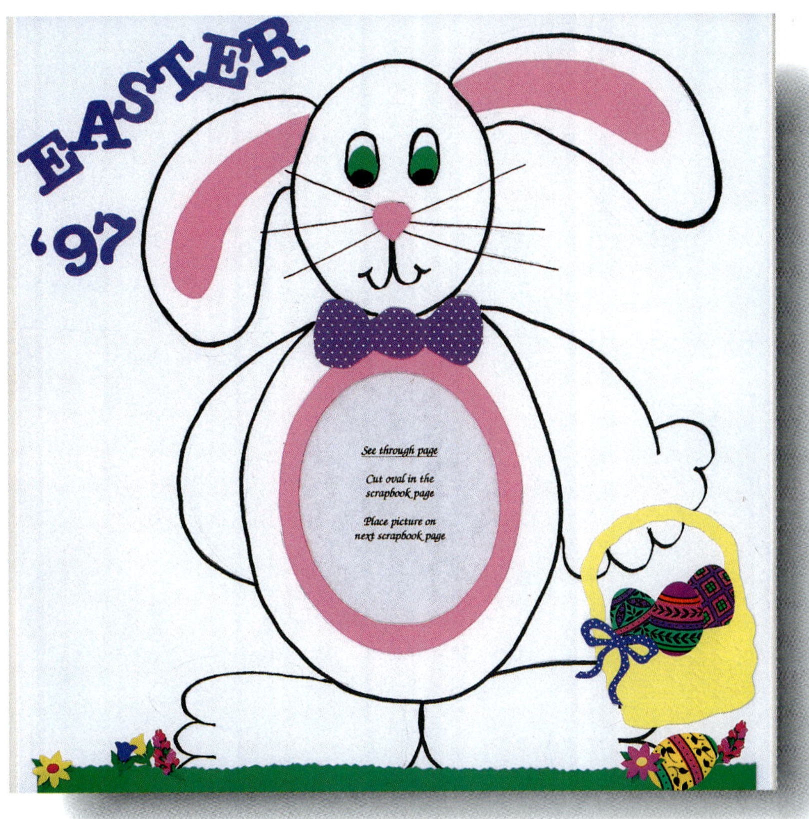
EASTER
'97
See through page
Cut oval in the
scrapbook page
Place picture on
next scrapbook page

Libby Ann's first photo shoot with Mollie. As you can see, she was very cooperative.

Father's Day

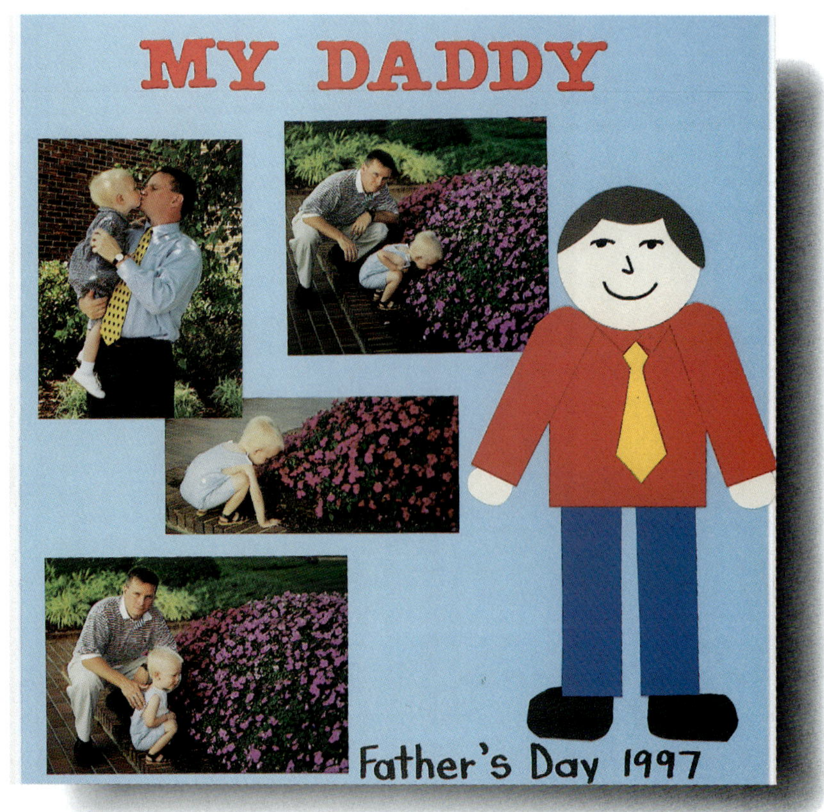

Happy
Halloween
TRICK OR TREAT!
Libby Ann helps Mr. Chet at
their Halloween Carnival.
My buddy
Kelsey W.
Cute
spooks
Adventureland
Costume Parade
Libby Ann & Kristin
This is no ugly duckling.
at Grand & Grandy's
TRICK OR TREAT!

Collin
was a black
cat on his
1st
Halloween.
He also had
his first
cold, but did
very well on his
"photo shoot." No
candy this year...
but we're sure
next year
will be
different.
Happy H'ween!
1996

Halloween

HAPPY
HALLOWEEN
TRICK OR TREAT!

Happy Halloween
Handing out candy
to Trick or Treaters
TRICK OR TREAT!

Halloween

Halloween
1997

Kelsey
The sucker goes in your mouth Colette, not in your eye.
Are those ears attached?
Kelsey checks out the loot!

Kiss Me Dahling!
xoxx
hugs ~n~ kisses
My little sweetie ~
xoxo
hugs ~n~ kisses
xoxx
xoxo
1987

CLOWNIN' AROUND!

The Greatest Gift
of All !

CHRISTMAS
'95

Merry Christmas!

MERRY
CHRISTMAS
WINTER
WONDERS

Christmas

1997
EMMA CAROLINE DENSON'S
FIRST CHRISTMAS

Ann's 1st Christmas! Libby
Santa's little helper! santa's little helper! Santa's little helper! santa
Libby Ann's 1st Christmas! Libby
Ho! Ho! Ho! Merry Christmas! Ho!
Ho! Ho! Merry Christmas! Ho!
Our best gift of all! Our best gift of all!
Our best gift of all!
To: The Olingers
From: Santa

Christmas

Christmas

Santa also came to Ann & Kathrine's house in California

Santa ate his goodies!

Ann Wilson

Ann and daddy (Rob)

While at the mall — might as well take
a ride on the carousel.

Robb's life time friend — Brian Mitchell
and wife Kerry.

Oh, what a busy day,
but not to busy to stop
and enjoy the quality time
to rock little Katherine.

This was our Christmas card that we sent to our friends this year. You weren't very happy about getting your picture made, but you still looked cute. Mimi made your outfit.

Christmas

LET * IT * SNOW * LET * IT * SNOW
*COLLIN'S FIRST SNOW
DECEMBER '96

The neighborhood was covered in snow and ice.
Snow Days
March 12-13, 1993
Its too cold outside, so Christina plays inside.

I can swim like a FISH
Libby Ann was two when she learned to swim!
Pop & BeBe's Pool! We ♡ it.

Fun at the pool
This was our first time to go to Point Mallard. You liked to play at the Duck Pond and slide down the slide. We went with Patrick Newsom and his parents. We had a great time.

Max
Abigail sliding
Gray at the Squirt Factory August 1997
Watch me, mama!
Cole, Chris & Abigail
Where's the soap?
Don't get wet!

Sprinkler Fun
May 16, 1993

Summer

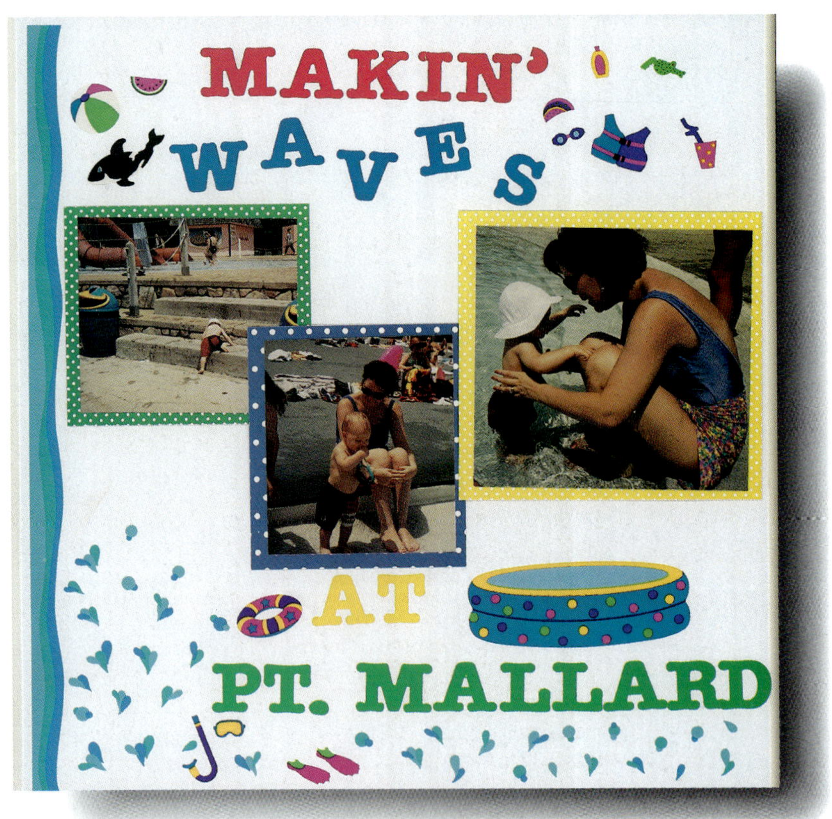

MAKIN'
WAVES
AT
PT. MALLARD

DIVE
~what
a sweetie~
~got the
sun in my
eyes~
~woops~
...i crack
myself up...
pool-
side
fun &
entertainment
...easssy... eassy...

Summer
Will loved to sit in Sam's bouncy seat and pretend like he was a baby.
Papa, Will, & Sam
Will & Sam

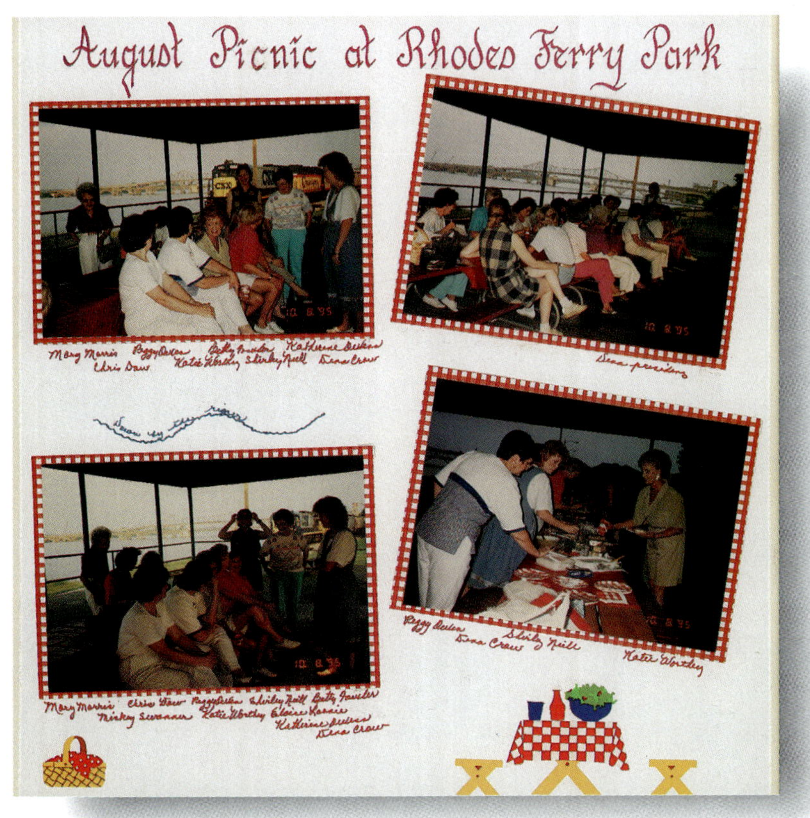

August Picnic at Rhodes Ferry Park

Summer

1997 Family Reunion

CAMP
Having a wonderful time...
Camping at
Joe Wheeler State Park
October 10-12, 1997
Our family, The Averitt's,
The Hills, The Humphries
The Owens, The Brewers &
The Kirchners.
wish you were here.
POSTCARD
POST
address only
to:
The Fun Times
123 Relaxing Ave.
Richer Life, State of mind
U.S.A.
or
Internationally
Saturday morning Breakfast
Pipe games

FALL FIELD TRIP
Ms. Ann & Ms. Robin's class.
The class took a field trip to Doyle
Whitlow's farm in Nashville. I went along,
as usual. We rode on a trailer thru' the fields.

Fall
1995
You got your red
wagon on your 1st
birthday. You loved
going for rides in
the wagon. Here
you are with Katie.
Mimi is taking you
for a ride. Uncle
Todd is holding
you and Katie.

Fall 1997

Getting Ready for a hayride.

Gray's Class Trip to Reeves
Peach Farm — Fall of 1997.
We ate crisp, green apples, had
a blast on a hayride And got
to pick out our own pumpkin.

Spencer Harvel

Abigail picks out her pumpkin

Learning to grind corn.

The Pumpkin Patch
October 18, 1977

1st & 2nd grade of Decatur Heritage

What a pretty leaf!

John, Jack, Francie, Caleb, Abigail, ?, Katelyn & Jenna Beth

Vibrant colors,
rustling winds,
amber leaves swept
down from trees,
Long brisk walks,
fireside talks...
Autumn is
a time for these.

Autumn Colors Warm the Heart
Abigail & Katelyn Free - Best Friends
Listening to the Story Teller
Petting the turtle at the Petting Zoo
Daniel, Christina, Abigail & Katelyn

Christina
Cullese
Crow

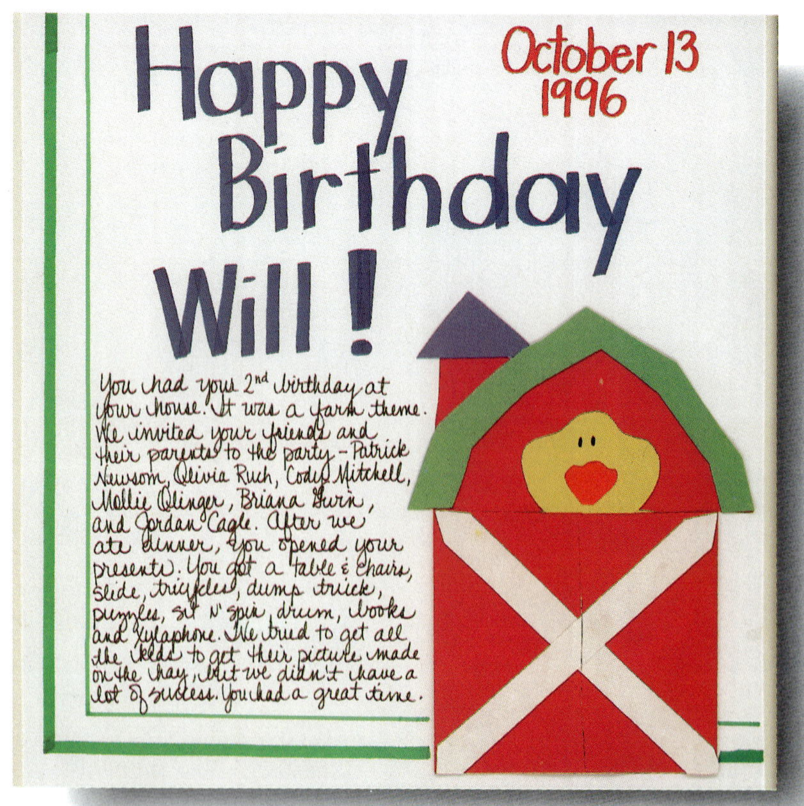

Happy Birthday Will !
October 13 1996
You had your 2nd birthday at your house. It was a farm theme. We invited your friends and their parents to the party - Patrick Newsom, Olivia Ruch, Cody Mitchell, Mollie Olinger, Briana Swin, and Jordan Cagle. After we ate dinner, you opened your presents. You got a table & chairs, slide, tricycles, dump truck, puzzles, sit n' spin, drum, books and xylophone. We tried to get all the kids to get their picture made on the hay, but we didn't have a lot of success. You had a great time.

COLIN

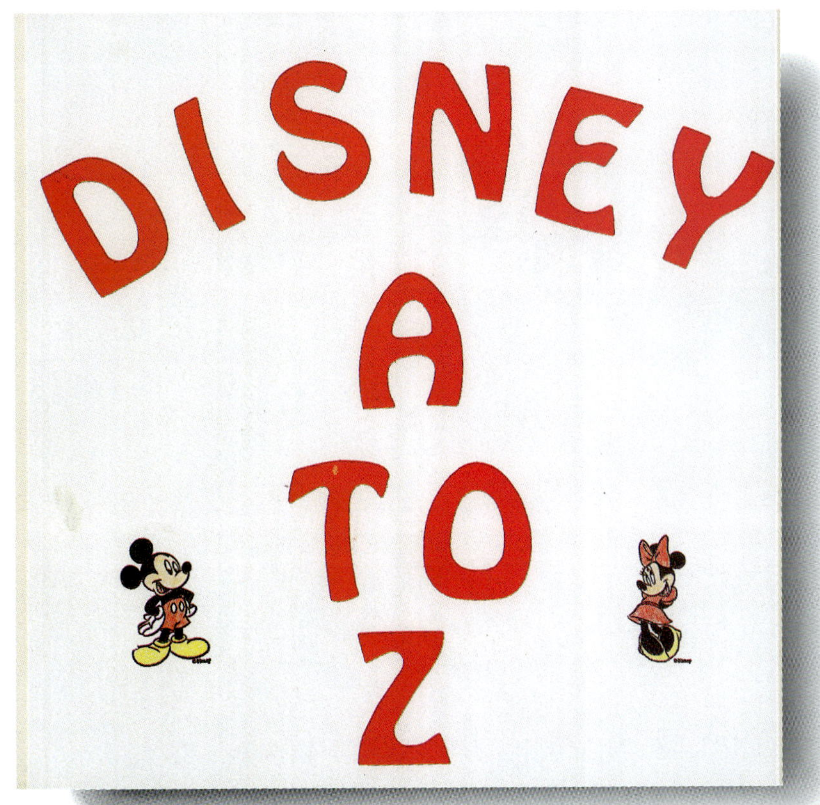
DISNEY
A
TO
Z

Yesterdays

GREECE
1997

Ann
Cullese
Wilson

With much love and joy
we are pleased to announce
the birth of
Ann Cullese
July 23, 1993
7 lbs.
19 1/2 inches
1:59 p.m.

Alison and Rob Wilson

May 22, 1996

July 5, 1996

Great
Grandaddy
and me

July 1996 ~
Aunt Leanne's Master's
Graduation

September
1996 ~ Grandaddy's
back yard
swing... whee!

May 1996 ~
Grammy and
Grandpapa's house
in matching bear and PJ's

Baby

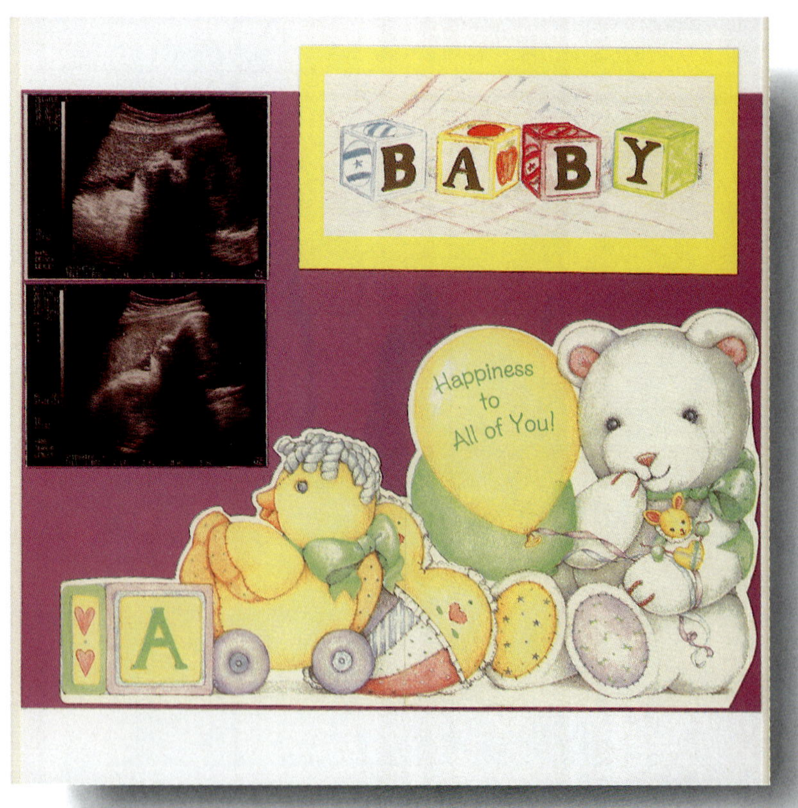

JON BRAXTON LEMLEY
5:17 p.m.
June 8, 1997
22"
8 lbs. 11 oz.

IT'S A BOY!

Great-Mamaw

I love my
May 1996
Great-Grandparent's
first visit ~ May 22nd, 1996
September 1996
Getting fed
by Mamaw

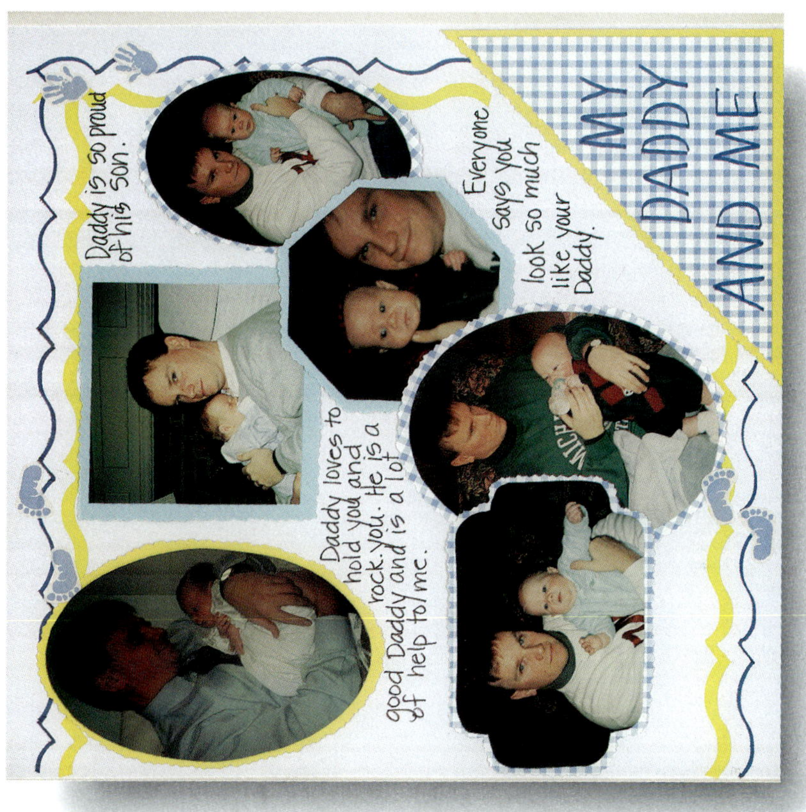
MY DADDY AND ME
Daddy is so proud of his son.
Everyone says you look so much like your Daddy.
Daddy loves to hold you and rock you. He is a good Daddy and is a lot of help to me.

MY MOMMY AND ME
Children are a blessing from God, and we were certainly blessed with you. You were a wonderful, happy baby. I loved to rock you, hold you, and kiss you.
You didn't like your bath very much at first.
I could not believe that you were finally here.

Baby

Going Home
Going Home
Going Home
Welcome Home. Christian and Mom
In the car seat of our 1989 Buick LaSabra
Going Home
Going Home
Going Home

Family & Friends
BeBe is proud of her third grandchild.
Another aunt Amy W.
Tadd & Martha visit from Nashville.
Finally an Olinger girl.
We had lots of visitors!
Drew and his mom came from Birmingham.

Splish Splash I was taking a bath long about a Saturday night. Rub a dub, just relaxing in the tub thinking everything was alright.
Mimi gave you your first, because Mommy was too nervous. I was scared that I might not do it right. You did not like your bath very much. You cried the whole time.
SpLISH SpLASH

Collin's
Bathtime!
TOOTHPASTE

Baby

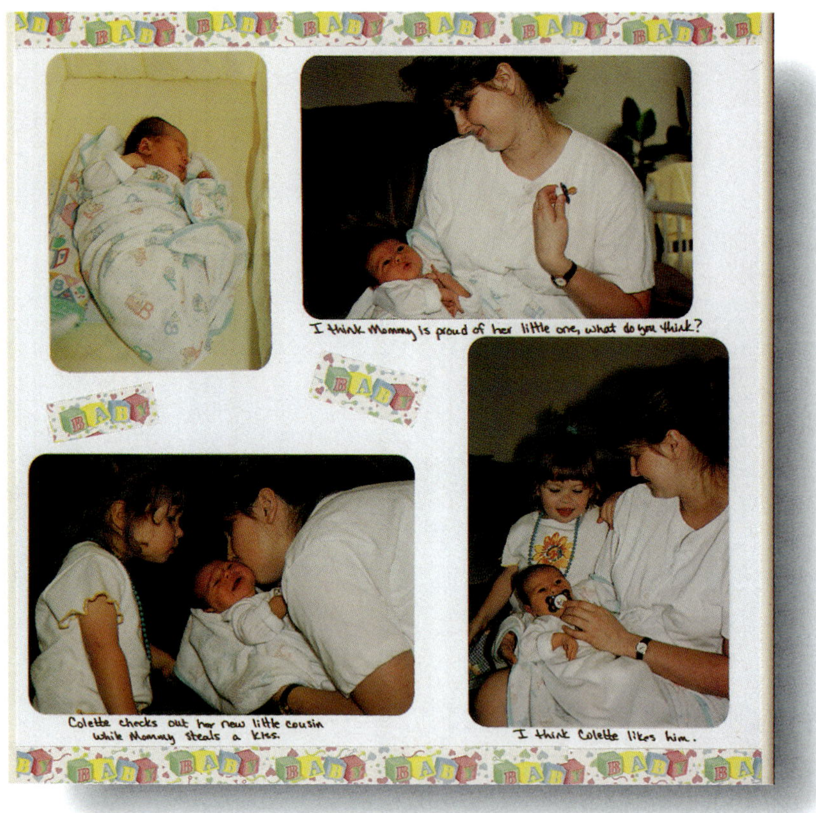

I think Mommy is proud of her little one, what do you think?
Colette checks out her new little cousin while Mommy steals a kiss.
I think Colette likes him.

Christina Crow
Homecoming Portrait
July 25, 1991

BRAXTON'S ROOM

LOOK WHO IS
HOLDING
CHRISTINA
Grand holding Christina
Daddy (John Crow) holding Christina
Grandaddy holding Christina

FIRST STEPS
Christina goes for Daddy's remote control
May 21, 1992

EMMA CAROLINE DENSON
7 MONTHS OLD
MAY 17, 1998
BUNNY LAND SEED CO.

DADDY'S
LIL'
SLUGGER
You're definitely an Olinger...
BALL was your first word

Collin in his baby bed
3 months old
3 mos.
NEW
KID ON THE
BLOCK

First time
to stand in
crib~
Collin's bedtime
buddy~ Bobby ~ often
found in this position!
STANDIN'
TALL
Collin learned that
if he stood up, we'd
"give him a bite"...
his favorite was
ice cream.
What a sweetie...
Sorry, Collin, Daddy's
out of food.

EMMA CAROLINE DENSON & MARY ANDERSON BROWN
MAY 3, 1998
(EMMA 6 1/2 MONTHS OLD,
MARY ANDERSON 8 1/2 MONTHS OLD)

Happy
Birthday!
Nail
Polish

Sarah, Melanie & Abigail
Princess Lei
Jordan
Sweet friends!
Manicures
Sarah is being
Pampered!
That feels so good, dahling!
Melanie & Sarah

PARTY

LET'S

Birthday

CHRISTINA
DAY
Christina's 1st Birthday

HAPPY 1st BIRTH
BABY'S 1st
BIRTHDAY!

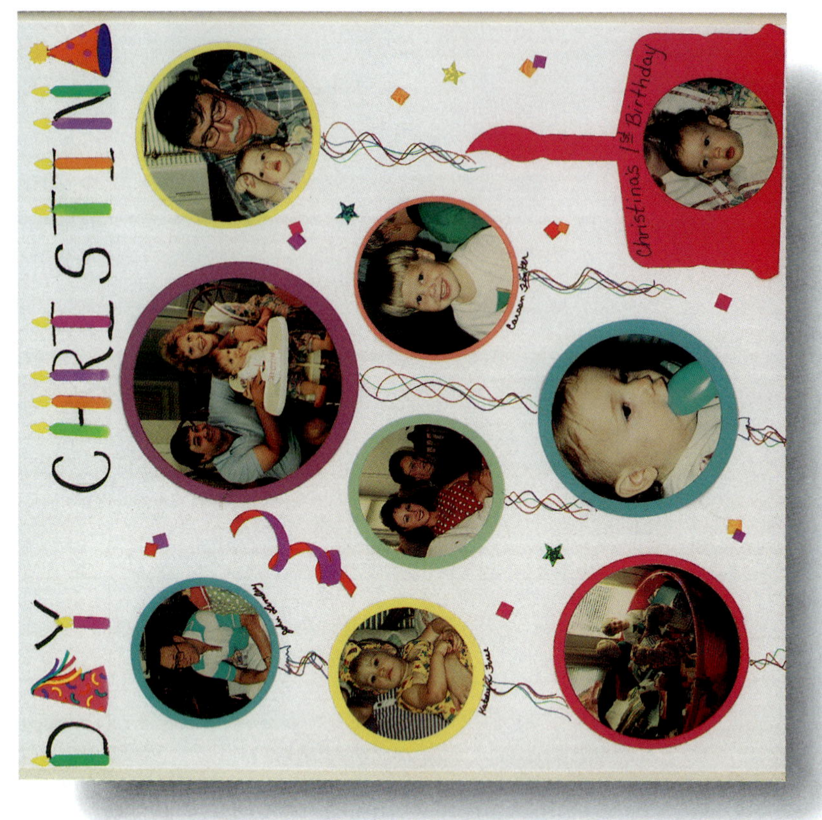

I love being a Cowboy!
Yum! I love cake and ice cream.
WILL'S FARM
Ready - Jump!
Grandmommy gave you a xylophone! You loved this toy. You would not let this toy...
We had your 2nd birthday at our house. We invited all your friends, and you had a great time!
We all ate on the deck. We had chicken tetrazini and salad. You were so excited that you could hardly eat!
Everyone is watching you ride your tricycle that Libby Ann and Mollie Olinger gave you! Watch out! Here I come!!

Bubba and Will playing the drums!
Crazy Uncle Buddy!
Mommy and Will blowing out the candles on your farm cake.
Will and Olivia Ruch playing in the ball pit.
WILL'S FARM
Cody is not sure about this!
Will is 2
HAPPY BIRTHDAY
October 13, 1996
Mommy had a hard time to get a group picture with Cody Mitchell, Patrick Newsom, Olivia Ruch and Patriana Will.
FARM

Birthday

DENA'S 29th BIRTHDAY

Over the hill Over the hill Over the hill Over the hill Over the hill Over the hill Over the
Opening presents at Mama Fay's
John and Christina
Vicki Smith, Christina & Chard

To Celebrate, We took Abigail and 5 of her friends to Profiles for hair-do's and Manicures. It was too much fun & the girls felt really special.
Abigail, Kacey & Caroline
Happy Birthday!
Making a BIG Wish!
Mommy lights the Candles.
This is the Best Part!
Sarah, Abigail, Kacey, Caroline & Jordan

For a Sweet Daughter's First Birthday
B·A·B·Y·S · F·I·R·S·T
B·I·R·T·H·D·A·Y

Birthday

HAPPY BIRTHDAY
Thomas Wilson (Grandaddy's) Birthday
March 26, 1992

Where's Trigger?
HOWDY YA'LL.
'The Apple Dumplin' Gang
Being a cowgirl ain't easy.
"GET OUT OF DODGE!!"
Marshall Humphries is in town.
Morgan Wallace's Birthday Party   Nov.' 96

The fun has begun...
Max is ONE!
Drey, Reid, Amanda & Jeanne Sessions, Seth, Mary Frances, Valerie & Jeremy
"Larry D", Kelly & Matthew
Melanie, Abigail & Kacey
Cardini is showing off her magic
Max & Uncle Phillip

Kelsey & Colette
3

CELEBRATE
We celebrated Grandmommy's 73rd Birthday at Mimi and Papa's house on Pinehurst. You loved looking at the candles. May 25, 1995
Hessie Faye Hawkins Bedingfield

Happy Birthday
Norma Hamilton, Dean, Jessie Odom, Bonnie Sellers

Children

Emma - Playmates
4-98
Oliver loves to sleep - especially with Emma.
3-98
Are these two laid back or what?
Emma & Oliver asleep in Emma's crib
Emma is closely checking Oliver out. She's getting gentler.
Oliver and Emma really like each other! He acts like a big brother.

Emma and Oliver
What a face!
Best Pals!
Oliver

Memories
Grandmommy took you for a ride.
Riding in the wagon with Olivia Ruch.
Having fun with Mimi!

Sweet
You helped Mimi blow out your birthday cake.
Your hair would stick straight up in the air.
You always wanted to show everyone.

Children

Busy as a bee-Bzzzz

Children

Collin Fuller
and
friend
CHOO-
CHOO

YOU ARE
MY SUNSHINE
Your Grammy made sure she "captured" your first Sunrise and Sunset. In July of '96, on your first trip to the beach, She took you out on the balcony (left) to watch the sun come up...
...Soon after, this sunset (right) was enjoyed on Grammy's back deck.

NINE IN THE BED AND THE LITTLE ONE SAID... ROLL OVER! ROLL OVER! EIGHT IN THE
THIS IS HARD WORK!
ROCK
-N-
ROLL
WHAT HAPPENS WHEN I FINALLY MAKE IT???
ROCK -N- ROLL... HMMM...
Juuust about to roll over--
August, 1996
4 months old
August, 1996
August, 1996

PLAYGROUND FUN
Christina showing off her new bikini!
A sunny day at Wilson-Morgan Park
March 28, 1993

Children

Sugar & Spice and everything nice, that's what little girls are made of? Sugar & Spice and
Too cool!!
Let II child just keeping pants up!
The next Michael Jordan!
Check out the dress
Chapped cheeks!!
Hanging tight
My ball costume
On the move!!
Ready for a bike ride with my teddy!
"Into" everything

Learning early to talk on the phone!
Singing on the potty
I'm bringing home a baby "bubble" bee
Won't my mommy be so proud of me!

Children

June 1996
Colette & Kelsey play at the lake near our house.
Colette & Kelsey holding hands
Kelsey
Sherry, Colette & Kelsey

FUN AT DAYCARE
Mexican day with Mrs. Susan.
On the playground
Nap time!

SPAGHETTI
TIME
Christina eating spaghetti on August 3, 1992.
Spaghetti is her favorite food.

Kiss me once
Kiss me twice
And kiss me once again.
Here you are kissing
Brianne Irwin and
Olivia Ruch. You were
a "kissing devil"!

Children

Playing in the turtle sandbox

Colette
Kelsey
Kelsey
Kelsey
Kelsey
Colette

1997
4-K
Decatur Heritage
Classmates:
Hannah Busing
Parker Hartsell
Blaze Towe
Brad McWhirter
Jackson Holland
Kayla Hurt
Kayla Miller
Andrew Cunningham
Mimi Temple
Tanya Parker
Jason Holt
School is Cool
Melissa Beard
ABC

School

MY YEAR AT ADVENTURE LAND
Everyday Activities
Teachers:
Ms. Joan
&
Ms. Judy
You learned so much this year!!
Gabriel
Gray Hunter Jacob Kelsey
Cole
'95 - '96
Libby Ann
Andrew Allison Zack
Morgan Claire
Christmas Program
Egg Hunt
Spring Program

Kacey receives her award.
Mrs. Jenny Harper gives you your award and tells you congrats on a great school year.
Kacey, Jordan & Jessica walk through the covered bridge.
Feeding the Ducks!
May, 1997
- Covenant's Sharp Arrow group took a field trip to Green Mountain State Park for a picnic and awards day. This was your last trip with the Sharp Arrow group.

..."MY" "CLASSMATES"...

Abigail learned
so much in this
class! She learned
to write her
name, and she
was also
interviewed for
The Decatur Daily
in their 3year
old section.
She was very
well liked by
all her classmates
and her teachers.

Bo Martin,
Mandy Sessions,
Melanie Ros, Abigail,
Sarah Lane, Conner
Slaughter, Reid Harris,
Trey Brewer,

Caitlin Free, Jordan
Doran,
Chris Humphries,
Sam

This geranium is just for you
with a note attached to say,
I love you very, very, much
and Happy Mother's Day

Adventureland 1995

Ms. Ann
&
Ms. Pam
(Mrs. Robin & Mrs. April)

Our Grandmother

Our Grandmother bakes
homemade bread, And is
very handie with needle
and thread.

She lets out hems, and darns
And patches; Sets the pins
up high, And hides the matches

Corrects our grammar, calls good
manners Art; Tells Bible
Stories she knows by heart.

Grows African Violets in a
dozen pots; Babysits us
And likes us a lot!

Gray & Mimi Inpu
1998

SCHOOL DAYS

Front Row: Libby
Ann Olinger, Cole Humphries,
Gabby Gray,
2nd: Morgan Wallace,
Kelsy Wallace,
Zac Ballard,
David Martin.

Max was born in
August, and you began
this class in September.
He began later in the
year, so we don't have
pictures of him at
Adventureland.

Gray had the best time in this
class! Playtime with all his friends
3 times a week. Ms. Joy was our
"nanny" during this time, so you considered
her your special teacher.

SPECIAL PEOPLE
IN MY LIFE

Ms. Joy
&
Ms. Beverly

Hannah Waugh, Taylor Teague, Zachery Heflin, Brett Wilson, Alix Wood, Abigail McBride. 2nd Row: Brett Graves, Jonathon Henslee, Mitchell Bazzel, Patrick Walsh, Brock Boyd + Chris Spicer. Coaches: Waugh, Wood, Graves & Spicer. Not pictured: Luke Allen, + Whitney Ball,

Vacation

my first trip to
the beach
destin, fl
july 1996

Will playing on the beach.
He loves to
play in
the
sand.
Julie and Sam

Beach
1996
When our family
went on vacation,
we went to Mimi
and Papa's house
in Pensacola, Fl.
You played in the
sand a lot and
loved to let the
waves run into
your legs. You had
to keep on your hat so
your bald head would not
burn.

PANAMA CITY
FUN! FUN! FUN!
You all enjoyed going to the Miracle Strip Amusement Park. I think
ya'll rode every ride that you could and Chandler loved playing the
baseball throwing game. Everybody's favorite ride was the bumper cars.
You all must have rode them five times.
Libby Ann also loved to drive the
cars.
Libby
Ann's
1st
Putt-Putt Golf game.
Pirate's Island
The beach and the pool were
the place to be during the day!

Vacation

Our family went to Gulf
Shores in May and
stayed on the beach. We
had a great vacation.
Will tried to
ride Todd's wave-
runner in the ocean
but a big wave
came and knocked
it over. You
decided not
to ride.

Vacation

THE SEA
Your favorite thing to do at the beach was to eat sand. You thought it was great!
Look at that belly!
You are so cool with your hat and sunglasses!
I can't get my shades, Mommy.
At the beach, you like to feel the waves roll up and touch your toes.

UNDER
This is your first trip to the beach - July 1995
Umm! Good
Mommy and Will
Katie, Julie and Will

ALL ABOARD
We rode the train at the zoo. It was Will's favorite!

Vacation

When you saw the elephant, you called him, "Dumbo."
You loved looking at all the animals.

LIMITED EDITION
1996 Olympic Torch Relay
Atlanta   A COMPETITORS PARADISE
GYM

EPHESUS
The Theatre where Paul spoke to the Ephesians
"Arcadian Way" where once Mark Antony and Cleopatra rode in procession
The Theatre had a capacity of 25,000 spectators
Chariot tracks down the stone road

The Temple of Nike
A view of the city of Athens. It was an overcast day.
Climbing up to the Acropolis
This guy wanted to charge us to take a picture with him, so when he turned around, we snapped a picture!

M IS FOR
MICKEY MOUSE
Disney

M IS FOR
MINI MOUSE

Colette
Mickey Mouse
Kelsey, Mickey & Colette
Kelsey & Colette get to meet
Mickey & Minnie Mouse at
the Madison Square Mall.

101 DALMATIONS

Vacation

C is for
Cinderella
February 10, 1998

D is for
Dinosaur
Daniel's favorite show was the dinosaur show at Epcot. It showed how energy is created, and began with the dinosaurs.
Christina and Daniel sit inside the skeleton of a dinosaur at Stage 54, which was a Jurassic Park exhibit in Universal Studios

H is for Haunted House
BOO!
Christina and Daniel's favorite ride

M is for
Mad
Hatter

Wedding

Aunt Bea and Warren's Wedding
May 26, 1990
Dayton, Ohio
Bea & Warren
Peggy & Ken Livingston
Aunt Julia & Aunt Bea
Dena helped at the reception
Linda and Frank Little

Miscellaneous

KLUANE MOUNTAIN RANGE

Miscellaneous

Christina received a swing set for her second birthday. She helped Daddy and Grandaddy put it together.

Christina took a picture of Daddy

Dena & Michelle Baker
getting things ready!

How many does it take to operate the bingo basket?

3 - One to instruct
One to crank the basket and
One to pick-up the spilled balls.

choosing the right prize

Margaret Ann thinks "what do I want?"

Miscellaneous

THE DECATUR DAILY, Wednesday, February 28, 1996

Patti Lovelady
ABWA Woman of Year

Woman of the Year

Patti Lovelady of Hartselle was selected as the American Business Women's Association's Woman of the Year. She is employed as a consumer products sales assistant at Cerrowire & Cable in Hartselle.

Mrs. Lovelady is the wife of Robert E. Lovelady Jr. and has one child. She is a graduate of Calhoun Community College and the University of North Alabama with a degree in marketing. She has served as ABWA chapter vice president, secretary and treasurer and program chairman, fund-raising co-chairman, education chairman and the Christmas party chairman. She is serving as treasurer and is part of the ways and means project.

Mrs. Lovelady is a PACT volunteer and is involved with Community Bible Study, Dreamweaver's Board and Decatur Cotillion. She is a member of Central Baptist Church.